Dear Parent:
Your child's love of reading starts here!

Every child learns to read in a different way and at his or her own speed. You can help your young reader improve and become more confident by encouraging his or her own interests and abilities. You can also guide your child's spiritual development by reading stories with biblical values and Bible stories, like I Can Read! books published by Zonderkidz. From books your child reads with you to the first books he or she reads alone, there are I Can Read! books for every stage of reading:

SHARED READING
Basic language, word repetition, and whimsical illustrations, ideal for sharing with your emergent reader.

BEGINNING READING
Short sentences, familiar words, and simple concepts for children eager to read on their own.

READING WITH HELP
Engaging stories, longer sentences, and language play for developing readers.

READING ALONE
Complex plots, challenging vocabulary, and high-interest topics for the independent reader.

ADVANCED READING
Short paragraphs, chapters, and exciting themes for the perfect bridge to chapter books.

I Can Read! books have introduced children to the joy of reading since 1957. Featuring award-winning authors and illustrators and a fabulous cast of beloved characters, I Can Read! books set the standard for beginning readers.

A lifetime of discovery begins with the magical words **"I Can Read!"**

Visit www.icanread.com for information on enriching your child's reading experience.
Visit www.zonderkidz.com for more Zonderkidz I Can Read! titles.

He holds the life of every creature in his hand.
—*Job 12:10*

He's Got the Whole World in His Hands
Copyright © 2008 by Zondervan
Illustrations copyright © 2008 by Molly Idle
Adapted from the lyrics of a traditional folk hymn.

Requests for information should be addressed to:
Zonderkidz, *Grand Rapids, Michigan 49530*

Library of Congress Cataloging-in-Publication Data

He's got the whole world in His hands / pictures by Molly Idle.
    p. cm. -- (I can read! Level 2)
  ISBN-13: 978-0-310-71622-8 (softcover)
  ISBN-10: 0-310-71622-5 (softcover)
  1. God (Christianity)--Omnipotence--Juvenile literature. 2. Children's songs, English--
    Texts. 3. Spirituals (Songs)--Texts. I. Idle, Molly Schaar.
  BT133.H47 2008
  782.25'30268--dc22

                                 2007034325

Editor: Betsy Flikkema
Art direction & design: Jody Langley

Printed in Hong Kong

08 09 10 11 12 • 5 4 3 2 1

I Can Read!

BEGINNING READING 1

He's Got the Whole World in His Hands

pictures by Molly Idle

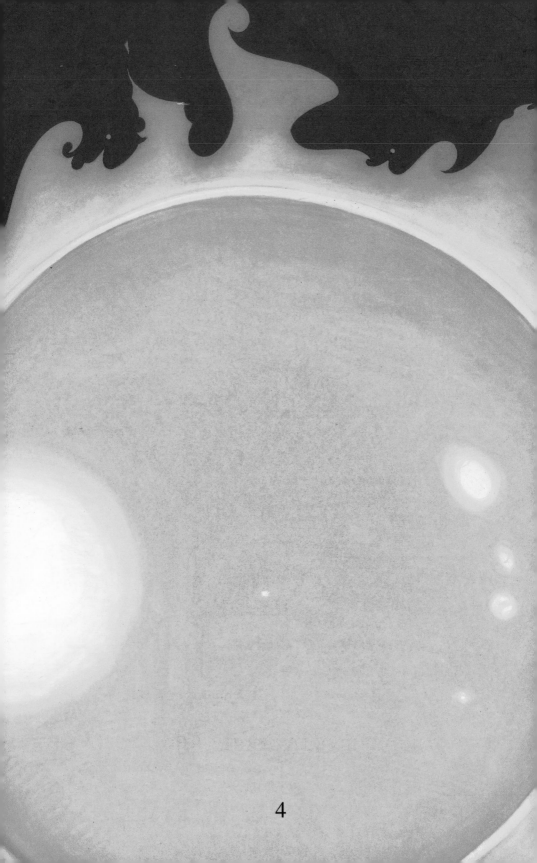

4

He's got the whole world

in his hands.

He's got the sun and the moon

in his hands.

He's got the earth and the sky
in his hands.
He's got the whole world
in his hands.

He's got the trees and the flowers
in his hands.

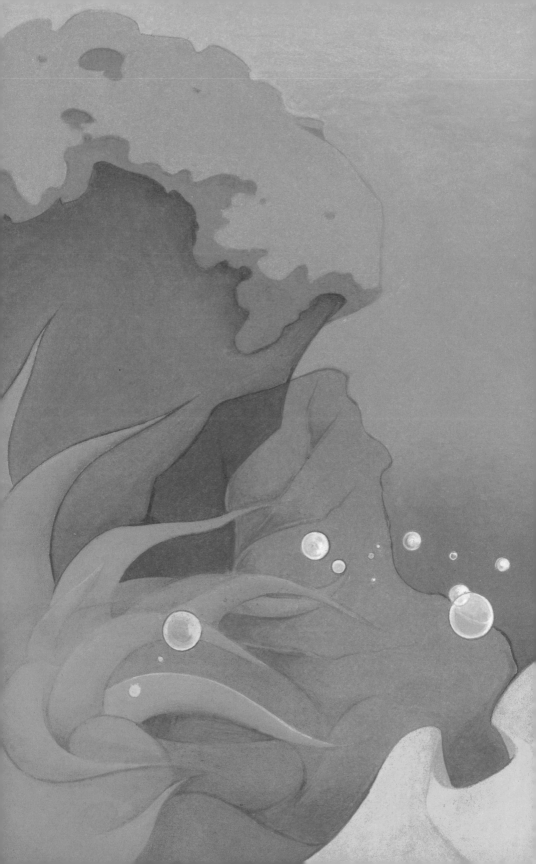

He's got the oceans and the rivers
in his hands.

He's got the wind and the rain

in his hands.

He's got the whole world

in his hands.

He's got the owls and the bluebirds
in his hands.

He's got the zebras and the lions
in his hands.

He's got the snakes and the turtles
in his hands.
He's got the whole world
in his hands.

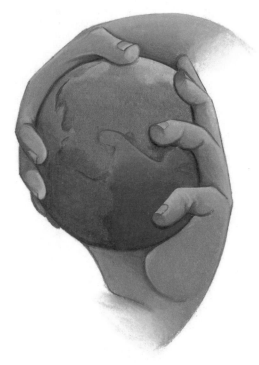

He's got the whales and the dolphins
in his hands.

He's got the lobsters and the crabs
in his hands.

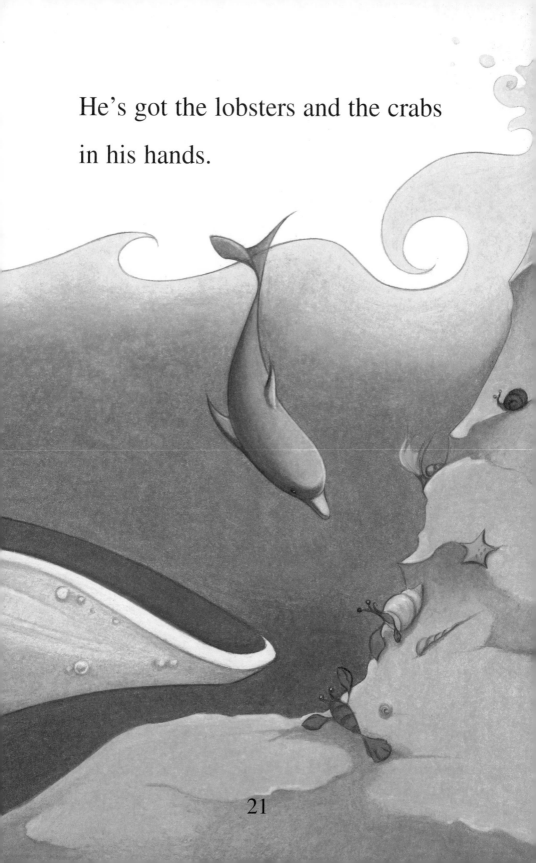

He's got the spiders and the bugs
in his hands.
He's got the whole world
in his hands.

He's got the grandmas and
the grandpas in his hands.

He's got the tiny little babies
in his hands.

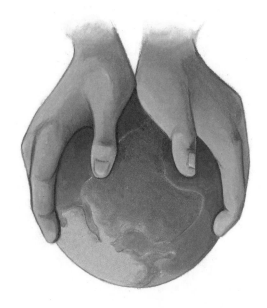

He's got the mamas and the papas

in his hands.

He's got the whole world

in his hands.

He's got everybody in his hands.

He's got you and me sister

in his hands.

He's got you and me brother
in his hands.

He's got the whole world
in his hands.

He's Got the Whole World
in His Hands

He's got the whole world in his hands, ___ He's got the

sun and the moon, ___ in his hands, ___ He's got the

earth and the sky ___ in his hands ___ He's got the

whole world in his hands.